ENDANGERED WETLAND ANIMALS

Dave Taylor

Toronto·Oxford·New York

Crabtree Publishing Company

ENDANGERED ANIMALS SERIES

Text and photographs by Dave Taylor

_____

For Mom and Dad

_____

Editor-in-chief
Bobbie Kalman

Editors
Janine Schaub
Shelagh Wallace

Type output
Lincoln Graphics

Design and computer layout
Antoinette "Cookie" DeBiasi

Color separations
ISCOA

Cover mechanicals
Diane Coderre

Printer
Worzalla Publishing

Published by
Crabtree Publishing Company

350 Fifth Avenue
Suite 3308
New York
N.Y. 10118

6900 Kinsmen Court
P.O. Box 1000
Niagara Falls, ON
Canada L2E 7E7

73 Lime Walk
Headington
Oxford OX3 7AD
United Kingdom

Cataloguing in Publication Data
Taylor, Dave, 1948-
  Endangered wetland animals

(The Endangered animals series)
Includes index.
ISBN 0-86505-530-0 (library bound) ISBN 0-86505-540-8 (pbk.)

1. Wetland fauna - Juvenile literature.
2. Endangered species - Juvenile literature.
3. Wildlife conservation - Juvenile literature.
I. Title. II. Series: Taylor, Dave, 1948-
The endangered animals series.

QL113.8.T38 1992   j591.52'9

Contents

The world's wetlands

Wetlands are found all over the world. They are wet, marshy places that are dry part of the year. Wetlands are often located near rivers and lakes, but they frequently develop in shallow depressions on grassy plains. All wetlands are important freshwater wildlife areas.

Millions of animals make wetlands their full- or part-time homes. Thousands of varieties of birds nest and raise their young in ponds, muskegs, and swamps. Many kinds of fish, reptiles, and insects also breed in wetlands.

Plenty of food and water

Animals living near wetlands often travel to these marshy areas for their daily drinks. Large animals, such as the rhinoceros and the crocodile, live in wetlands because these areas supply plentiful sources of food. People, too, depend on wetlands.

Ecological wonders

Wetlands help clean and enrich our oceans and lakes. In fact, a wetland plant called the water hyacinth actually removes pollution from water! Wetlands contribute to the fertility of soil in surrounding areas by adding minerals to it, thereby resulting in good farmlands. Wetlands are also valuable as tourist areas for bird watchers and others who are interested in observing wildlife.

Draining the wetlands

Sadly, wetlands are disappearing all over our planet because they are often located in regions that people want to farm or use for building houses. Many of the world's wetlands have been permanently drained to make room for people. As a result, millions of wetland animals are now endangered because there is no place for them to live or find food.

Although saltwater seas and oceans contain ninety-eight percent of the world's water, all living things need fresh water. Wetlands, such as the marshy areas shown below, support an abundance of wildlife.

Animals in distress

In recent years, people have forced many kinds of animals to struggle for survival. Hunting, farming, and the loss of wilderness areas have made life difficult and sometimes impossible for thousands of species of animals.

Worldwide conservation groups have developed various terms to describe animals in distress. Animals that are **extinct** have not been seen in the wild for over fifty years. Animals referred to as **endangered** are likely to die out if their situation is not improved. **Threatened** animals are endangered in some areas where they live. **Rare** animals are species with small populations that may be at risk.

A concern for all animals

There is a concern for all animals living in the wild. Even if some species are not yet threatened or endangered, they may lose their lives because of pollution or loss of their homes. There is hope, however. Due to the efforts of conservation groups, many animals that once faced extinction are now surviving in healthy numbers again.

(opposite page) The false gharial is a type of crocodile that lives in the rivers, lakes, and swamps of the Malayan Peninsula and Borneo. It has a very thin snout. It is hunted for its skin.

(right) Wood storks are the only kinds of storks found in North America. Unfortunately, most of their wilderness homes are gone because people are draining swamps for farming and building. A few protected areas have been set aside for wood storks, but their numbers remain low.

(below) Trumpeter swans are the largest swans in North America. Their population decreased as the prairie ponds in which they built nests were drained to provide more wheat-farming land. Today trumpeter swans are protected, and their populations are once again increasing.

The great egret

Great egrets are sometimes called common egrets. They are found all over the world. They can be seen stalking fish in the marshes of Africa's plains, resting in trees in Florida's everglades, flying over the Amazon River in South America, spearing fish along China's rivers, or roosting in Australia's swamps.

Egrets belong to the heron family. They have long legs for wading in water and through tall grasses, and long necks and sharp beaks that enable them to spear fish after fish!

Hat feathers

A hundred years ago, bird hunters were shooting egrets by the thousands for the long, lacy, white feathers that egrets grow during mating season. These feathers, called **plumes**, were used to decorate women's hats. Over 190,000 egrets had to be shot to get one year's supply of hats.

Slaughter during breeding

Egrets grow plumes during the mating season and use them in their courtship dances. They keep these beautiful feathers during the breeding period and then lose them after all their young have been raised. Since egrets only have plumes when they are having their young, hunters destroyed many eggs and chicks while they were shooting the parents. For each year that hats with egret feathers were in fashion, 600,000 birds died, including adults and babies.

Regrets about egrets

Fortunately, hat feathers went out of fashion before the birds became extinct. It was partly due to concern over the fate of these birds that two great conservation efforts were started. The Audubon Society began as a group of people who wanted to raise public awareness about the dangers facing egrets. The second effort was the National Wildlife Refuge Program, which resulted from the work of the Audubon Society. This program provides land for many endangered animals.

Hope in numbers

Today, great egrets are again a common sight. There are, however, a few varieties that are in danger because their wetland homes are being destroyed. Like other wetland creatures, their survival depends on the efforts made by people to preserve wetland areas.

Height: 37-41 inches (94-104 centimeters)
Where it lives: Wetlands throughout the world

The survival of the egret is a real success story. It shows that there is hope for all animals.

The white pelican

White pelicans are among the largest birds found in North America. They have a wing span of almost 10 feet (3 meters)! Like all pelicans, they have a long bill with a pouch. This pouch serves as a net to scoop up fish.

White pelicans nest on inland lakes in or near North America's great plains, as far north as Canada's Northwest Territories and as far east as the Ontario-Manitoba border. Most of these birds fly south to the Gulf of Mexico in winter. Although they spend their winter months catching food from the salty ocean, they prefer fresh lake water.

The catch-all bill

Many fishing companies use pelicans as their symbol because these birds are such successful hunters. They swim along slowly, watching and listening for fish. Then, at the right moment, they dip their bills into the water and scoop up their catch. They also scoop up a pouchful of water, which must drain away before the birds can swallow their fish.

Deadly DDT

In the 1950s the pelican population fell rapidly. Once a common sight flying over western lakes and rivers, pelicans were sighted less and less often. They were being rapidly destroyed by a new farming chemical called DDT. Farmers sprayed the chemical on crops to prevent insects from eating their produce. When it rained, the DDT washed off the plants and slowly made its way into nearby rivers and lakes where it was absorbed by tiny water creatures. The tiny creatures were then eaten by small fish, which in turn, were eaten by bigger fish. Each time a bigger animal ate a smaller one, the chemical also entered its body.

Fragile eggshells

When a pelican ate a fish, it also consumed highly concentrated doses of DDT. Although the DDT was not strong enough to kill the adult birds, it affected the eggs of the female pelicans. The egg-shells were so weakened by DDT that they broke when they were laid, and no baby pelicans were born.

Out of danger

By 1960, scientists finally realized that DDT was killing birds and affecting the whole food chain. A ban was placed on the use of this dangerous chemical. It took over twenty years before the pelican population was large enough that the species was considered "out of danger."

Height: 54-70 inches (137-178 centimeters)
Weight: 24 pounds (11 kilograms)
Where it lives: North America, from northern Canada to the Gulf of Mexico

Pelicans live on rivers, lakes, and seacoasts in temperate and tropical regions of the world.

Pelicans are clumsy on land, but they are graceful in flight.

The massasauga rattlesnake

Massasauga rattlesnakes are secretive creatures that avoid people. They are such experts at hiding in marshy grasslands and in crayfish tunnels that for many years no one knew how many of these snakes existed.

Seeking out snakes

As many wetlands were being drained, scientists began to wonder whether massasauga rattlesnakes were becoming endangered. These snakes were steadily being killed by people who built farms, houses, and marinas. A few years ago,

scientists asked cottagers and campers to report massasauga-rattlesnake sightings. They discovered that there were more snakes than was originally thought, but that these creatures still needed protection to survive.

An undeserved reputation

Most people have seen movies that show rattlesnakes rattling, lunging, and delivering deadly bites. In nature, however, this is not the way rattlesnakes commonly behave. Massasauga rattlers avoid people and would never chase anyone! The rattle sound made by rattlesnakes is created by loosely connected shell-like pieces in their tails. Making the sound is a way of saying, "You are too close. Stay back!"

Rattlesnakes cannot jump at people; they can only strike as far as their curled-up necks can reach—perhaps a hand length or two at most. It is true that a few people have died from massasauga-rattlesnake bites, but these are rare occurrences.

rattle tip

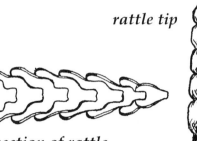

cross section of rattle

Respecting rattlers

If you are walking in rattlesnake country, wear boots and pants with loose-fitting legs to protect you from the rare possibility of a bite. If you do hear a snake rattling, do not move quickly because this may frighten the snake. Step back and walk slowly around the rattler. If it is left alone, it will go on to hunt the frogs, toads, mice, and birds that make up its diet.

> **Length**: 20-40 inches (51-102 centimeters)
> **Where it lives**: Eastern and central North America

Massasauga rattlesnakes shed their skins many times during their lives. They do not, however, shed the rattle segments at the tips of their tails. Each year a segment is added to the rattle. Although these sections sometimes break off, it is safe to estimate that rattlers with many sections are old snakes.

The hippopotamus

The name hippopotamus means "river horse"— but hippos are not horses at all! They are relatives of the pig family that have become more at home in the water than on land. Once ashore, the bellies of hippos almost touch the ground.

At times, the stumpy legs of the hippos seem nearly overpowered by their hefty bodies. In the water, however, these piglike creatures can gracefully prance along the bottoms of lakes or rivers because the water supports their massive weight. Hippos are also powerful swimmers and can remain underwater for several minutes.

Long-time targets

Once hippopotamuses lived all over Africa. In the past, hippos were hunted for their meat. Although they are still killed for meat today, they are mostly hunted for their ivory teeth. To escape the hunters, hippos stay only in areas with reeds, so they can remain hidden. The only large herds of hippos left in the world are found in Africa's national parks. In unprotected areas, their population is falling rapidly.

Hippos have fearsome teeth! Each tooth can weigh up to 6 pounds (almost 3 kilograms) and be as long as 24 inches (61 centimeters). Hippos are hunted for their ivory teeth.

Night grazers

Most photographs of hippopotamuses show them wallowing in mud or submerged in water. These are their day-time activities but, at night, they leave the water to graze. They do not eat water plants but, instead, feed on a variety of inland grasses. By daybreak, all hippos return to the water. Not only does the water provide safety, but it also keeps the hippos cool and their skin healthy. Without water, hippo hides would dry out and crack.

Those fearsome teeth!

Each herd of hippos is ruled by one bull. This bull maintains his territory by using his teeth in fights with other hippos. These fights can be quite nasty and sometimes last up to an hour. Most hippos have scars on their hides from these battles.

Hippo harmony

Males fight fiercely to maintain separate territories, but herds of up to 100 females and youngsters live in harmony. Cows give birth to calves weighing about 60 pounds (27 kilograms). Their babies are born away from the herd, and the mothers do not rejoin the other hippos until their calves are two weeks old. Crocodiles are the biggest threat to hippo babies.

Height: 54 inches (137 centimeters)
Length: 9-14 feet (2.7-4.3 meters)
Weight: 3,000-7,000 pounds (1360-3175 kilograms)
Where it lives: South of the Sahara Desert in Africa

(above) Crocodiles swim and feed in the water, but they come out to bask in the sun. (below) Young crocodiles eat mainly insect larvae and small shellfish. As they get older, fish and meat make up their diets. Some adult crocodiles even eat baby crocodiles!

The Nile crocodile

Crocodile numbers have fallen greatly since the 1950s, and these creatures are now in need of greater protection. They have been shot for their skins, which are made into shoes, purses, belts, and even leather coats! Many crocodiles are killed because they are a threat to people. Crocodiles can be dangerous and are best avoided.

Necessary predators

The killing of crocodiles has a negative effect on the African wildlife community. Crocodiles help keep African waters clean by eating dead animals that would otherwise pollute the lakes and rivers. Their trails along the banks make paths for other animals to use and, as predators, they help keep herd animals healthy. They kill the weak and sickly and thereby control the number of animals in herds. When people shoot thousands of crocodiles, they are disturbing the natural food web.

Attentive mothers

Mother crocodiles guard their nests and chase off animals that try to dig up the eggs. Crocodile eggs are buried under loose sand and plant material, which keep them warm and hide them. When hatching time arrives, the babies make a peeping sound, and the mother crocodiles dig them up. Mother crocodiles then carry their babies to the water in their mouths. Mothers stay with their young in the water until the babies can catch their own food. Baby crocodiles eat insects and small fish. They grow about a foot each year. They are fully grown around the age of fifteen and may live to be over fifty.

Drag, twist, and gulp

Adult crocodiles swim slowly towards the bank with only their eyes and noses showing above water. They grab animals that come to the water for a drink and then drag them into the river or lake. Once crocodiles have a large animal in their jaws, they cannot just eat it because they cannot chew! Instead, they twist their catch around in the water until they can rip off chunks of meat small enough to swallow. Crocodiles also eat stones. These stones stay inside their stomachs and help grind up the large chunks of food that they have swallowed.

> **Length**: 16 feet (4.9 meters)
> **Where it lives**: African rivers and lakes south of the Sahara Desert

Crocodiles eat dead animals that would otherwise pollute rivers and lakes.

The Indian rhino

The Indian, or one-horned, rhino has rolls of skin that overlap, making the animal look as if it is wearing a protective covering. Although the hides of rhinos resemble armor, their skin does little to protect them from the bullets of poachers, who kill them for their horns.

Hairy horns

Rhino horns are not made of bone but of many hairlike fibers. These fibers are massed together to form a hard horn that grows out from a bony patch on their foreheads. Both males and females have horns that can measure up to 18 inches (46 centimeters)! Rhino horns have been valuable trade items for centuries. In some Asian countries, rhino horns are believed to carry medicinal powers. Horns are ground into powder and are then used in many different folk medicines. A good-sized horn can be worth well over $20,000. Even though rhinos are protected, their horns are so valuable that poachers still prey on these animals.

Living in nature reserves

Today there are fewer than 1,600 Indian rhinos left in the world. Most live in the Kaziranga Nature Reserve in north-eastern India. Wild Indian rhinos can only be found in the marshlands surrounding the Brahmaputra River. India's growing human population forces rhinos to occupy smaller and smaller habitats.

Gentle plant eaters

Although Indian rhinos look ferocious, they are gentle plant eaters most of the time. Indian rhinos have developed special lips that are quite long and narrow. They use these lips to grab branches or eat large mouthfuls of grass. Although Indian rhinos have very poor eyes, they possess an excellent sense of smell that helps them locate their favorite plants.

Living alone

Indian rhinos are usually solitary animals, but sometimes up to thirty animals gather in one grazing area. Indian rhinos do not have large territories and can usually be found in the same area day after day. Pairs of rhinos are made up of mothers and young.

Caring for baby

After giving birth to a baby that weighs approximately 50 pounds (23 kilograms), a mother stays with her calf for three to four years. The new hippo can live to be fifty years old. Its natural enemies are crocodiles and tigers.

Height: 56-73 inches (142-185 centimeters)
Length: 122-150 inches (310-381 centimeters)
Weight: 3,500-4,850 pounds (1588-2200 kilograms)
Where it lives: India and Nepal

Male rhinos often damage or break off their horns during battles with other males. These fights usually take place when rhinos are defending their territories or during competitions for the right to breed with a female.

The eastern hognose snake

Eastern hognose snakes are gentle and harmless. They are now rare for two reasons: 1. People kill them because they believe that these snakes are dangerous. 2. The places where these creatures used to live have been destroyed by the building of houses and cities. There are fewer and fewer sandy beaches where hognose snakes can make their homes and hunt toads and frogs.

Hognose snakes are endangered partly because of their excellent acting abilities! Although they themselves are not dangerous, they are experts at pretending to be other kinds of dangerous snakes.

Pretending to be deadly

Hognose snakes do not have rattles, but they can rattle their tails as if they were rattlesnakes. They move their tails

quickly back and forth against dried leaves, making the feared rattlesnake sound. Hognose snakes also pretend to be cobras. They rear up and flatten their necks to resemble a cobra that is about to strike. There are no cobras in North America, but most people do not realize this and react as they would to a "deadly" snake. People who fall for the tricks of hognose snakes often end up killing these creatures. Animals leave the snakes alone. Hognose snakes also play dead by rolling over onto their backs and sticking their tongues out the sides of their mouths. People who pick up these "dead" snakes make a humorous discovery. If you return "dead" hognose snakes to the ground on their bellies, they flip over onto their backs again.

> **Length**: 20-33 inches (51-84 centimeters)
> **Where it lives**: Eastern North America, from southern Ontario to Florida

The roseate spoonbill

Roseate spoonbills, or "pinks," as they are sometimes called, were hunted to near extinction for their pink feathers. In the early 1800s, there were thousands of roseate spoonbills. In 1939, when there were only thirty left in the United States, laws were passed to protect them from hunters. By 1950, the population had increased to 400.

Mysterious decline

Today, spoonbills are no longer considered endangered, but their population has decreased, and the reason for the decline is not known. It may be caused by the destruction of their habitats.

Food in shallow marshes

The shallow-water marshes that disappear when land is drained for agriculture are especially suited to the bird's wide bill. Spoonbills catch small insects, worms, and fish by sweeping their long, flat bills back and forth in shallow water or mud.

Looking after their young

In the winter, roseate spoonbills nest in the mangrove swamps of the West Indies, Florida Keys, and South America. They mate with one partner each season (a different one each year). Each female lays two to four reddish-brown eggs, which take twenty-three to twenty-four days to hatch. The pair stays together until, at seven weeks of age, the young start to fly.

Molt and fly

After nesting, the adult spoonbills **molt**, which means their old feathers fall out and their new feathers grow in. When some birds molt, they cannot fly because they lose their feathers all at once. Spoonbills can always fly because they lose their feathers over a long period of time.

Height: 32 inches (81 centimeters)
Where it lives: Gulf coast of North America, Central America, and South America

When spoonbills fly, they extend their legs and neck gracefully. They are a beautiful sight!

The alligator

In the 1950s alligators were in danger of disappearing from North America. These big reptiles were killed for their skins, which were used to make purses, belts, and shoes. Alligators were further threatened when people took over their wetland homes. Even after alligators were given protection as endangered animals, poachers still shot a large number each year.

Change for the better

The people concerned with the survival of alligators helped change the fate of these reptiles in two ways: 1. Game wardens were employed to catch and arrest poachers. 2. Alligator farms were set up to raise alligators especially for their skins. These farms are like other farms, except alligators are raised instead of cows and pigs. Because alligator farms could produce thousands of these huge reptiles, the price of alligator skins dropped in the fashion market, and it was no longer worth the risk for poachers to hunt alligators in the wild. As a result, wild alligators grew in number once again and have become a common sight in southern wetlands.

Welcome pond makers

Florida's cattle ranchers were happy to see the number of alligators grow again. They discovered that these mighty reptiles played an important part in drought control. Alligators dig deep, wide holes in the earth. These holes fill up with water and become ponds.

Alligators do this to attract prey to their watering holes and to ensure that they have water during dry periods. Cattle use these ponds when water is scarce. When alligators were rare, however, few of these ponds could be found during droughts.

Caring mothers

Female alligators make huge nests of rotting grasses in which they lay and cover their eggs. Unlike many other reptiles, alligators do not abandon their young; they stay close to protect the nest from invaders. Baby alligators break out of their shells with the help of a sharp, but temporary, tooth on their snout. The peeping babies are gently carried to the water in the mighty jaws of their mothers.

Hunted again

Today, alligators may once again be legally hunted under strict rules. The greatest danger they face, however, is Florida's growing human population. Perhaps the only place where alligators will continue to survive are in national parks such as the Florida Everglades.

Length: 6-18 feet (1.8-5.5 meters)
Where it lives: The southern coast of the United States

Alligators have broad, short heads, whereas crocodiles have longer, thinner heads. Alligators cannot chew their food. Instead, they rip chunks of meat off their prey and swallow these pieces whole. Sometimes alligators stash their prey underwater for several days to "tenderize" the meat. They find rotten meat easier to tear than a fresh carcass.

The osprey

Ospreys are fish-eating birds that soar gracefully in the sky above shallow bays and marshlands. They circle over the water until they spot a fish near the surface. Then they dive, feet first, into the water and almost disappear with a huge splash. With a few powerful wing beats, they take off again, clutching the fish in their talons.

Dangerous DDT

During the 1950s osprey populations dropped due to the use of DDT, an insecticide that was widely used by farmers. The chemical was washed into lakes and rivers, where it was taken in by fish. Ospreys ate large quantities of poisoned fish, and they themselves became poisoned. The recovery of ospreys began when DDT was banned.

Ospreys can once again be seen in many European and North American wetlands. The present-day threat to ospreys is the destruction of the marshes and swamps on which these birds depend.

Sharing space

Ospreys have little fear of people. They can often be seen diving into the shallow waters in cottage country and building their nests on poles near marinas, homes, or even in parking lots. As long as people share their space with ospreys, these birds will be around for a long time.

Annual nesters

Ospreys return to the same nest year after year. Since these birds may live up to forty years, they keep some nesting sites for several decades! Female ospreys lay two or three eggs. Hatchlings are fed by both parents and leave the nests when they are about seven to eight weeks old. Osprey chicks usually fly to a saltwater bay or shallow lake a long way from home. After remaining at this location for two or three years, they return to the area where they were born.

Height: 22-25 inches (56-64 centimeters)
Where it lives: All continents except Antarctica

Ospreys build their nests in tall trees, on the ground, or on cliff edges. The nest looks like a large pile of sticks. The spotted feathers of osprey chicks camouflage them well in their nest.

Preserving wetland areas

Wetlands can be found all over the world. They are being drained and replaced by homes, factories, and farmlands. Almost all are endangered habitats.

Hazardous wastes

For hundreds of years, people used rivers to get rid of their garbage and sewage. In many places, people still dump waste material into rivers. This pollution then flows into lakes and wetland areas and slowly begins killing the animals there, too.

Make sure that you and your family are not contributing to the pollution of wetland areas. Reduce, reuse, and recycle waste so that hazardous substances do not get emptied into rivers and streams. The chemicals in items such as lawn fertilizers, paints, and thinners can destroy wildlife.

Conservation groups

There are many conservation groups working to educate people about the importance of wetlands. Some of these groups buy wetland areas or pay farmers to leave them alone. One North American group even creates new wetlands by using dynamite to blast shallow holes into the ground. These holes then fill up with water and become ponds.

Passing the word

You can help wetlands by making posters, writing stories, and talking about wetlands so that others can learn how important they are. Many communities organize yearly clean-up activities. Local groups choose a day to clean up a marsh, stream, or pond. Find out about your community's efforts. You will get muddy, have fun, and learn a lot just by being in a wetland area.

Visitor support

One of the best ways to help preserve wetland areas is by visiting one! Not only will you find a wetland area an interesting place in which to observe wildlife, but the interest you show will help maintain that area as an important reserve!

Glossary

ban The official forbidding of something

cobra A large poisonous snake found in Africa and Asia

concentrated Denser; stronger

conservation Protection from loss, harm, or waste, especially of natural resources, such as wildlife

DDT An insecticide that is poisonous to humans and animals

decline A decrease, as in amount

drought A long period of dry weather

ecological Relating to ecology

ecology The relationships of living things to their environment and to each other

endangered Threatened with extinction

everglade A large area of low, marshy land covered with tall grasses

fertility A state of being productive

fiber A fine, threadlike substance

folk medicine The traditional medicine of a common people of a region or country

food chain A group of plants and animals that is related in that each is food for a larger animal

food web A number of interrelated food chains

game warden A public official who enforces hunting and fishing laws

habitat The natural environment of a plant or animal

hatchling A recently born young bird

herd A group of large animals

heron A wading bird with a long slender neck, bill, and legs

insecticide A chemical used for killing insects

mangrove Tropical evergreen trees found in marshy areas

marsh Low, wet land covered with grasses

molt To shed feathers, hair, or skin in preparation for new growth

muskeg Wet, spongy ground

national park An area of land maintained for public use by the government

plains An area of flat land

poacher A person who hunts illegally

pollute To make impure or dirty

pollution The state of being polluted

population The people or animals of an area; the total number of individuals living in a particular area

predator An animal that captures and eats other animals

prey An animal hunted by another animal for food

recycle To make waste material suitable for reuse by treating or processing it

reduce To make smaller

reputation The way in which people think of a person or thing

reserve Land set aside by the government for a special purpose

Sahara Desert The largest desert in the world. It is found in North Africa.

soil fertility The productivity of the soil

species A group of related plants or animals that can produce young together

swamp Low land flooded with water and usually covered with dense vegetation, such as trees and grasses

threatened Endangered in some parts of its habitat

Index

3 4 5 6 7 8 9 0 Printed in USA 1 0 9 8 7 6 5 4 3